Meditations for the Grieving

Herald Press
Meditation Series

Meditations for Adoptive Parents
by Vernell Klassen Miller

Meditations for the Expectant Mother
by Helen Good Brenneman

Meditations for the Grieving
by Richard L. Morgan

Meditations for the New Mother
by Helen Good Brenneman

Meditations for New Parents
by Gerald and Sara Wenger Shenk

Meditations for the Newly Married
by John M. Drescher

Meditations for Single Moms
by Susanne Coalson Donoghue

Meditations
for the Grieving

RICHARD L. MORGAN

Herald Press
Scottdale, Pennsylvania
Waterloo, Ontario

Library of Congress Cataloging-in-Publication Data

Morgan, Richard Lyon, 1929-
   Meditations for the grieving / by Richard L. Morgan.
      p. cm. — (Herald Press meditation series)
   ISBN 0-8361-9320-2 (pbk. : alk. paper)
   1. Consolation. 2. Bereavement—Prayer-books and devotions—English. I. Title. II. Series.
   BV4905.3.M67 2005
   242'.4—dc22

                                    2005022005

MEDITATIONS FOR THE GRIEVING
Copyright © 2005 by Herald Press, Scottdale, Pa. 15683
            Published simultaneously in Canada by Herald Press,
            Waterloo, Ont. N2L 6H7. All rights reserved
Library of Congress Control Number: 2005022005
International Standard Book Number: 0-8361-9320-2
Printed in the United States of America
Cover art by Esther Rose Graber

10 09 08 07 06 05   10 9 8 7 6 5 4 3 2 1

To order or request information, please call
1-800-759-4447 (individuals); 1-800-245-7894 (trade).
Web site: www.heraldpress.com

For my brother, Howard Campbell Morgan,
who has taught me more about grief
than all the books I could ever read.

Contents

LIFE BEGINS AGAIN

Author's Preface

It is impossible to comprehend the anguish and sorrow of loss until death comes to someone you love. With the death of a loved one, a part of yourself has died, too. In Margaret Craven's novel, *I Heard the Owl Call My Name,* a young priest named Mark Brian learns from the Native Americans of the Northwest that when a person is about to die, the owl calls their name. The owl has called the name of my parents, stepmother, sister, niece, cousins, and many friends. The owl has called the name of many of your loved ones, too. Or perhaps this is the first time. We never truly know when death may come.

During more than fifty years of pastoral ministry, I have been with many families who grieve. I am deeply indebted to those who shared their broken hearts with me. They have touched my life with grace and truth. As I entered into their struggles of faith, I heard unforgettable stories of how they dealt with loss and found new beginnings. Every ending has a beginning. Their stories inspired me to write these meditations for others who mourn.

These meditations of Scripture, poetry, personal and other devotional thoughts were written to help you as you work through your own grief. I hope and pray that whenever death enters your life, robs you of loved ones, and launches you into uncharted waters of the grief journey, these meditations will offer spiritual help.

> Blessed are those who mourn,
> for they shall be comforted.
> *Matthew 5:4*

In some of his final words to Timothy, the apostle Paul talks about his death, that the time had come for his departure. The word *departure* is a nautical term; it suggests a ship that has been marooned on the shore, but the rope is now flung off, the anchor lifted, and the ship moving out of harbor into the wide and boundless sea. Here we are anchored to the hardships and heartaches of life. In the death the gangway is raised, the anchor is weighed, and we set sail for the glorious shore.

Paul sees death as moment of new adventure, not as a time for sadness or defeat. It is not like an old half-ruined wreck of a ship limping to port; rather is a ship which has cast off the ropes which bind us to this world to sail unknown waters to a new home. It is scary to think that as a ship leaves the port into the deep and cannot envision the future harbor, so death takes us from a life we know to an unknown destination. Yet, it is only on the sea that the ship can fulfill the purpose for which it was made. It is only through the deep waters of death that we find our true home with God.

> SUNSET and Evening Star,
> and one clear call for me!
> And may there be no moaning of the bar,
> When I put out to sea.
>
> But such a tide as moving seems asleep,
> Too full for sound and foam
> When that which drew from out the boundless deep
> Turns again home.
>
> Twilight and evening bell,
> And after that the dark!
> And may there be no sadness of farewell
> When I embark.
>
> For 'tho from our bourne of Time and Place
> The flood may bear me far.
> I hope to see my Pilot face to face
> when I have crossed the bar.
> *Alfred Lord Tennyson*

When Death Comes

Behind the altar on the east wing of the chapel of a
Trappist monastery high up in the Rocky Mountains,
on the right side of a stained glass window of Our Lady,
there hangs a simple wooden cross.
It will stay there until it is taken down to mark
the grave of whichever brother is the next to die.
Until then it hangs on the wall so that whenever
the monks turn and face the altar they also turn
and face this very simple and immediate symbol
of their own death.

Esther DeWaal

Death Never Takes a Holiday

But God said to him, "You fool! This very night your life is being demanded of you. And the things which you have prepared, whose will they be?"   *Luke 12:20*

It is appointed for mortals to die once, and after that the judgment.
Hebrews 9:27

The rich farmer in Luke 12 expected to expand his property, increase his wealth, and enjoy all the pleasures he so richly deserved. He was unaware that life was uncertain and that that night he would face a rendezvous with death. Death never takes a holiday. The grim reaper can walk into anyone's life at any time, like a thief in the night. Many times I have thought of the words of Robert Browning's poem, "Just when we're safest, there's a sunset touch / A fancy from flower-bell / Someone's death. / A chorus ending from Euripides, / And that's enough for fifty hopes and fears."

We are like the women who watched Jesus die from afar. We push thoughts of death out of our mind and keep it at a comfortable distance. Then someone dies and life is thrown into disarray. The death of a loved one takes center stage, and the roles we must play are not always clear.

Grief is awkward and uncomfortable. The word *grief* means "heavy." It may well be the heaviest weight a person must bear. Death is the unwelcome intruder that stole your loved one and robbed you of love and joy. Life will never be the same. When all the family and visitors have departed, you find yourself surrounded by a strange silence. It is like being in a yawning cavern with no light in sight, or going on a journey with no help from MapQuest. You get out of the house to see family and friends, but always the emptiness awaits you.

John O'Connor, a Celtic priest, said it well, "Death is a lonely visitor. After it visits your home, nothing is ever the same again . . . there is an absence in the house. . . . Something breaks within you then that will never come together again." Like it or not, prepared or not, your journey into grief has begun.

Lord Jesus, you were acquainted with grief. You wept aloud when your friend Lazarus died. We feel so bereft and alone without our loved one, but you have a part in this sorrow that tears our heart.

With you a part of me hath passed away;
For in the peopled forest of my mind
A tree made leafless by this wintry wind
Shall never again don its green array.
Chapel and fireside, country road and bay,
Have something of their friendliness resigned;
Another, if I would, I could not find,
And I am grown much older in a day.

George Santayana

But hark! My pulse like a soft Drum
Beats my approach, tells Thee I come;
And slow howe'er my marches be,
I shall at last sit down by Thee
The thought of this bids me go on,
And wait my dissolution
With hopes and comforts, Dear (forgive
The crime) I am content to live
Divided, but with half a heart,
Till we shall meet and never part.

Henry King

Till Death Do Us Part

> So Rachel died, and was buried on the way to Ephrah, (that is Bethlehem), and Jacob set up a pillar at her grave; it is the pillar of Rachel's tomb, which is there to this day.
>
> *Genesis 35:19-20*

Once I stood at a grave in the dead of winter; the tent poles were clanging in the wind. Sad faces were glued on the casket. Suddenly, the grieving widow cried out, "Don't leave me! Don't leave me! I want to die too." She seemed inconsolable and overcome with grief. Sad to say, she did grieve herself to an early death in a matter of months.

The loss of a spouse is a devastating loss. Philosopher Arnold Toynbee, in his "Reflections on My Own Death," suggested that true love is possibly proved by the wish of a person to outlive his love, so that the loved one is spared the anguish and grief. Jacob knew that distressful grief. Rachel was Jacob's greatest love, and he looked forward to spending the rest of his life with her. But instead he found himself building a pillar at her grave and journeying on to Canaan alone, still numb and in shock. No doubt he wished he could die and be buried with Rachel.

When you lose a spouse, you lose part of yourself. Even the presence of children and friends cannot soften the pain or replace the loss. You ask yourself what will happen now that you are alone, without your life companion. Your spouse was the one who was always there for you. They listened as you shared with them the events of your day. When things went wrong, they were the first to hear you and offer their presence. You have a great fear of living alone, that something might happen to you and no one would care or notice.

A widow told me, "I learned that the word *widow* comes from a Sanskrit word meaning 'empty.' Well, my life has been empty for some time. I know I have my children, but life just isn't the same without him." Make no mistake, time can help the grief, but it does not heal the loss and pain.

Compassionate God, you empathize with us when our spouse dies. We recited the words of our wedding vows, "Till death do us part," but we never thought it would end so soon. Help us, Lord.

I come back from the cemetery riding up front in the hearse,
back now empty of the casket. . . .

There comes a day when everyone comes back
from the cemetery except me.
I wonder what will happen then. . . .

As for my work, if I die tonight there will be Church next Sunday,
and all of that is as it ought to be,
others going on with the work which I have done,
doing it as well or better.

I am left thus with this lesson, that any difference my life makes
must be the difference it makes to me and not to others.
Now, let me see, what difference do I want my life to make for me
before the day which is to be
when everyone comes back
from the cemetery except me?

John D. Burton

When a Parent Dies

> Abraham breathed his last and died in a good old age, an old man and full of years. . . . His sons Isaac and Ishmael buried him in the cave of Machpelah. . . . And Isaac breathed his last; he died and was gathered to his people, old and full of days, and his sons Esau and Jacob buried him.
>
> *Genesis 25:8-9; 36:29*

What a striking contrast in the burial of two fathers. Isaac and his half brother, Ishmael buried their father, Abraham. If either of them said anything while they leaned on their shovels, with their old father lying six feet deep beneath them, those words were never recorded. They were probably silent, still alienated by memories of the past. Abraham had banished Ishmael and his mother, Hagar, to the desert. Unresolved conflict between the sons only made the distance greater. But they did make one final rendezvous to bury their father.

On the contrary, I imagine Esau and Jacob embracing as they met to bury their old, blind father Isaac. God had helped Esau overcome his resentment at the way Jacob had cheated him of his birthright and blessing. Reconciled, they both grieved the death of their father.

Ordinarily our parents precede us in death, but regardless of their age their dying leaves a void in our lives. The death of a parent often carries a mixture of positive and negative feelings. At times you may feel relief, especially if your parent had lingering and painful suffering. Death is a blessing. On the other hand there are natural feelings of sadness and nostalgia. Mourning is much more complex when a relationship with a parent ends in estrangement.

I recall a touching moment as I stood with a family while their aged father was dying and gasping for breath. He seemed so forlorn and hopeless as his wife and daughter grasped his hand. Finally they said, "Daddy, it is all right to let go. We will always love you." His fragile hold ended, symbolic of giving up and letting go. He died in peace.

Gracious Jesus, you loved Mary and Joseph, and must have mourned when Joseph died. You understand our sadness when our parents die. Give us assurance they are at peace and one day we shall see them again.

Here she lies, a pretty bud,
Lately made of flesh and blood.
Who, as soon, fell fast asleep,
As her little eyes did peep.
Give her strewings; but not stir
The earth, that lightly covers her.

R. Herrick

MOURNING GLORY

Down passages we choose to take
Through the labyrinth of life,
Moving toward the open door
To the garden of fertility
In fiery passion, awoke a sprout, a bud
Certain to blossom forth.
A light turned on within me
And revealed the doorway to life.
In conception, I was born again
But this time living, not dying.

Eighth times the moon lit up the night
But the ninth time fell in the shadow
And the bud had to blossom
in the dark of the moon.
Then light went out in my soul;
Pain, separation, and all in the blackest night.

The shadow slowly slipped away
As stealthily as it had come;
And my bud is planted on a hill,
a victim of the night.

For an instant I had felt and understood
The dawn of the spring of new life.
Now I am as old and hard as stone.

Maria

Mourning Glory

I am weary with my moaning;
every night I flood my bed with tears;
I drench my couch with weeping.
My eyes waste away because of grief.

Psalm 6:6-7

Maria was one of my best students in a religion class I was teaching. I knew her baby was due soon, and everyone was excited for her. Then I heard the tragic news. During labor the fetal monitor wrapped around Maria's abdomen showed that the baby's heart abruptly stopped. An emergency caesarean section was done in order to rescue the baby. Despite the efforts of the medical staff, the baby was stillborn.

In several weeks Maria returned to class. She seemed morose and sad, and still in shock. Later, she wrote a poem that vividly described her pain entitled, "Mourning Glory" (see page 18).

Her poem reflected the agony of stillbirth. Statistically, there is one stillbirth for every eighty live births. Often the cause of death is completely unknown.

Maria left school after the first semester and it has been years since I have seen her. I wrote her a letter and expressed my condolences but never heard from her. I have long wondered how her life turned out. Did she recover and have other children? God only knows.

Loving Father, you care for us beyond our fondest hopes and dreams. You hurt when we hurt, and feel our pain. Bless all parents who lose a child at birth. May their sorrow find comfort in your presence.

Holy God, when you come to us in the darkness of our grief,
 we are able to see you more vividly than during
 any of the brightest moments of our lives.
It is in the darkness and silence
 that you make yourself known to us most completely.
Help me endure my moments of darkness,
 secure in the knowledge that you are always beside me.

Ann Dawson

There is no flock, however watched and tended,
But one dead lamb is there!
There is no fireside howso'er defended,
But has one vacant chair!

The air is full of farewells and dyings,
And mournings for the dead;
The heart of Rachel crying,
Will not be comforted!

Let us be patient! These severe afflictions
Not from the ground arise,
But oftentimes celestial benedictions
Assume this dark disguise.

We see but dimly through the mists and vapours.
Amid these earthly damps,
What seems to but sad, funereal tapers
May be heaven's distant lamps.

Henry Wadsworth Longfellow

A Sharp Sword

> The king was overcome with emotion. He went up to his room over the gateway and burst into tears. And as he went, he cried, "O my son Absalom! My son, my son Absalom! If only I could have died instead of you! O Absalom, my son, my son."
>
> *2 Samuel 18:33 (NLT)*

It was a moment of heartbreak. Bobby had left with his high school friends to attend a basketball game. On their return, on a miserable rainy night, the car careened off the road, hit a tree, and Bobby was thrown from the car and instantly killed. No one else was injured. At the funeral service, his mother was grief stricken, and during the hymn, "Abide with me, fast falls the eventide," she suddenly jumped from her pew, and threw herself over Bobby's coffin, sobbing and crying, "My God, my God, why did you let this happen?"

King David's son, Absalom was a thorn in David's flesh, but he was also the apple of his eye. David told his general, Joab, to go easy with Absalom, even if he had led a rebellion against his father. But Joab murdered Absalom. When Joab broke the news to David, it broke his heart, and he cried the words that have echoed down the centuries, "If only I could have died instead of you!" He meant it of course. David would gladly have died for his son, and many parents who lose a child feel the same way.

The death of a child at any age, for any reason, is a shattering moment. Ann Dawson, in her wonderful book, *A Season of Grief,* describes her heartbreak after her son's death, "When Andy died, and my world turned upside down, I was terrified at the intensity of my pain." She recalls the strange words of Simeon to Mary, the mother of Jesus, who was probably overwhelmed with love for this new child of hers, "And sorrow, like a sharp sword, will break your own heart" (Luke 2:34-35). Parents who lose a child know that sword.

Jesus, tender shepherd who loves all the little lambs of your flock, give comfort to all parents who have lost their children, and with them their hopes and dreams for them. May they know they are safely gathered in by you, the Good Shepherd.

My heart was utterly darkened by this sorrow
and everywhere I looked I saw death.
My native place was a torture room to me,
and my father's house a strange unhappiness.
And the things I had done with him—
now that he was gone—became a frightful torment.
My eyes sought him everywhere, but did not see him;
and I hated all places because he was in them,
because they could not say, "Look, he is coming,"
as they did when he was alive and not absent.
I became a hard riddle to myself. . . .
Nothing but tears were sweet to me
and they took my friend's place in my heart's desire.

> *St. Augustine, on hearing of the*
> *sudden death of his friend,*
> *Adeodatus*

I've found a Friend, O such a Friend!
He loved me ere I knew Him;
He drew me with the cords of love,
and thus He bound me to Him.
And round my heart still closely twine
Those ties which nought can sever,
For I am His, and He is mine,
Forever and Forever.

> *James G. Small*

When Friends Die

How I weep for you, my brother, Jonathan! Oh, how much I love you!
And your love for me was deep, deeper than the love of women!
2 Samuel 1:26 (NLT)

The loss of friends is difficult at any age. They leave a vacant place in our lives which no one can fill. Florida Scott Maxwell wrote, "We live in a limbo of our own. Our world narrows. . . . Friends die, others move away, some become too frail to receive us and I become too frail to travel to them . . . we tend to live in a world of our own making, citizens of Age, but otherwise nameless." Although these words express the feelings of loss of an older person, they resonate with us all.

David wept over the death of Jonathan, his covenant brother and soul friend. Jonathan's father, King Saul, consumed by jealousy and torn by moods of depression and paranoia, tried to kill David whom he viewed as a dangerous rival to his throne. Repeatedly Jonathan had sided against Saul and was there to warn David and help him escape. When Jonathan died, David's lament is one of the most touching poems in the Old Testament.

After the death of several friends and relatives in succession, the poetess Emily Dickinson wrote these words in a letter to a friend. "The Dyings have been too deep for me, and before I could raise up my Heart from one, another has come." Months ago that happened to me, as a valued friend, a wonderful pastor, my mentor, and a college roommate all died within the span of a few weeks.

In the Celtic tradition there is a Gaelic term for friendship, *anam cara* (soul friend). This is a person with whom you can share your innermost self, one who truly accepts and understands you. When you lose an *anam cara* by death at any age, it is as if a part of you had died.

When our friends die, we cherish even more friends who are alive. But we also discover that these losses deepen our relationship with God, the eternal Friend, who will always be present with us.

Eternal Father, Friend always, when the circle of our friends begins to shrink as death takes its toll, we feel their loss keenly, for the bell of death tolls for us some day. Surround us with your Presence.

A little boy was dying with leukemia. One night his mother read the story of King Arthur and the knights of the round table, and how many of them died fighting for the cause. Suddenly the little boy asked his mother, "Mommy, what does it mean to die?" She ran to the kitchen, desperately trying to find the words, and then returned and answered his question. "Son, do you remember when you were a little boy and we took a long trip to see Grandpa and Grandma, and you would fall asleep in the car?" "Oh yes," replied the boy, "And when I woke up the next morning I was in my own bed because Daddy's strong arms carried me there."

"Well, son," his mother replied, "This is what it means to die. We fall asleep and wake up in the morning in God's house, where we belong, because a loving Father carried us there."

Author Unknown

Where Did Daddy Go?

Remember, O Lord, what has befallen us . . . We have become
orphans, fatherless, our mothers are like widows.

Lamentations 5:1, 3

It was the middle of the night and I was roused from sleep by the ominous ring of the telephone. Groggily, I picked up the phone, and a frightened voice said, "I am Twila's mother. Her husband was burned to death tonight in a horrible accident, and they had to rush my daughter to the hospital for fear she would give premature birth to her baby."

Hurriedly, I dressed and went to their home where Brenda, age 7, and Greg, age 2, sat in the parlor looking bewildered. Their grandmother looked at them and said, "Children, the preacher has something to say to you." All my seminary classes and theology went out the window. Fumbling for words I simply said, "Children your father has died, and God has taken your father to be with him." Greg never understood until later that his Daddy had died, but Brenda looked at me and said, "Where is my Daddy?"

It has been over fifty years since that moment of heartbreak, but her question has haunted me ever since.

All too often we say platitudes to children to soothe their pain. Phrases like, "Well, God has a garden in heaven and he took your Mommy because he needed the best flower he could find." Or, "God loved Daddy and wanted him in heaven." A child may think, "God loves me and Mommy, too. Is he going to take us to heaven?" We need to be direct and make children know that God is love and is never the cause of a bad thing that happens.

It is hard for little children to express their grief in words. At times they can express their feelings by drawing pictures, writing stories, or in other creative ways. My seven-year-old granddaughter, Brannon, grieved when her first grade teacher died with cancer. She visited the funeral home, but said little. Later she composed the words and music of a beautiful song for her teacher on her violin, and shared the music at school.

Jesus said, "Let the little children come to me and do not stop them." Help us to be gentle and kind when our children face death. Give us the right answers to their questions.

Death is carrying us on one arm, while the other flings back heaven's
door to welcome us back to the blazing hearth of our first home.
While those, inside, having arrived before us, rush to the door
like glad children, saying, "They're here."
Death has a bad name on earth, but in heaven
it is a homecoming party every time the door opens.
God does not forget the earthbound children, sad and left behind,
God leave the party early to enter into their despair and
let them get ready for their own parties someday.

Author Unknown

Lord, If You Had Been Here

> Martha said to Jesus, "Lord, if you had been here, my brother would not have died. . . ." When Mary came where Jesus was and saw him she knelt at his feet, and said to him, "Lord, if you had been here, my brother would not have died."
>
> *John 11:32-33*

Two sisters, so different in personality and temperament, were united in grief when their brother Lazarus died. Martha the server and activist, went out to meet Jesus on the road, while Mary stayed home, probably praying in her room. Yet both expressed the same complaint, "Lord, if you had been here, our brother would not have died." Their words expressed their belief that Jesus could have cured him. Not only does it appear from the biblical accounts that the three siblings were good friends, but the sisters relied on Lazarus to be the man of the house at Bethany; he was their breadwinner.

Once I listened as a woman poured out her heart after the death of her brother. She was a widow, with no children, and her brother was her only family. He managed her finances, and took her to the grocery store and medical appointments. Now she had no one except a few friends. She sighed as she said, "I am the last one left in my family. There is no one with whom I can share family memories. I feel like the last twig on a barren tree. What will I do?"

I was very close to my sister, Mary. She was the one with whom I bonded as a child. We maintained our relationship through the years and kept in close touch. She was the one who instigated family reunions and often jokingly said, "We'd better get together soon before we meet at one of our funerals." Little did I imagine she would die first, a victim of cancer.

It is significant that Jesus did not come immediately to console Martha and Mary, but waited two days. We will have to wait much longer before we see "those angel faces, whom we have loved long since, and lost awhile." Our faith is in the risen Lord who reunites us in a better home in the eternal family of God.

Jesus, Lazarus was not your blood brother, but he was your soul brother. You wept loud tears at his grave. Whether we mourn when a brother or sister dies or experience grief later, surround us with your compassion.

Alzheimer's is a particular type of disease
because it confronts us with sustained dying,
and is an inescapable reminder that we all will die.
We cannot forget this reminder of our shared mortality
because we are living with dying each day.

David Keck

I don't know where I am or where I am going.
I stare a lot and the moment is just that.
I fear for not knowing what to do next.
For the simple little things I try to do my best.
I look in the mirror and cannot see me,
And when I do I want to be free.
I go back and enjoy some of my past.
I am not sure if even those thoughts will last.
Please understand me because of who I have been,
And understand where I am going and the fog I am in.

Lynn Algeri, writing as the voice
of her mother after she died from
Alzheimer's disease

The Funeral That Never Ends

I have been dismissed as one who is dead,
      like a strong man with no strength left;
They abandoned me,
      and I am as good as dead.
I am forgotten.

Psalm 88:4-5 (NLT)

A friend whose wife had Alzheimer's disease once told me, "I grieved for her many years before she died, as I watched her disappear into nothingness. My heart broke when the day came when she didn't even know who I was." He added, "Just imagine you had a photograph of your wife, and it became fainter and fainter until all that remained was a blank page. She died before the funeral."

Called the "funeral that never ends," persons with Alzheimer's disease or other forms of dementia mirror death itself. It is one thing to lose cognitive functions and one's memory. It is difficult when persons with Alzheimer's disease become aware of what is happening and lose hope. But the last stage is the worst, when the person needs total care, and at times is regarded by some as no longer a human being.

Psalm 88 describes the suffering of a person cut off from life. He is as good as dead, forgotten. So it is with victims of Alzheimer's disease. They are society's forgotten souls, ordinarily locked into dementia units or nursing homes, with little contact with the world. Other than nursing assistants and family members, they are "dismissed as one who is dead."

We need to reach out with love to family members of persons who suffer this disease. They need our support and the assurance that God cares and never forsakes their loved one or them. In fact, Jesus went "outside the city gate," and always reached out to those shut in by society. I am sure if Jesus were present today you would find him with these forgotten souls of our age.

Lover of lost souls who left the ninety and nine to seek and save the one lost sheep, give us grace to leave our comfort and reach out to those shut in by this dreaded disease. May our compassion for family who sit and watch their loved ones die before the funeral go beyond words to action.

When sorrows come, they come not as single spies but in battalions!

William Shakespeare

For all the saints, who from their labors rest,
Who, Thee, by faith before the world confessed.
Thy name, O Jesus, be forever blest.
Alleluia! Alleluia!

Thou was their rock, their fortress, and their might.
Thou, Lord, their captain in the well-fought fight,
Thou in the darkness drear,
their one true light,
Alleluia! Alleluia!

O blest communion, fellowship divine!
We feebly struggle, they in glory shine;
Yet all are one in Thee,
for all are Thine.
Alleluia! Alleluia!

And when the strife is fierce, the warfare long
Steals on the air the distant triumph song,
And hearts are brave again and arms are strong/
Alleluia! Alleluia!

From earth's wide bounds, from ocean's farthest coasts,
Through gates of pearl streams in the countless host,
Singing to Father, Son, and Holy Ghost.
Alleluia! Alleluia!

William Walsham Howe

Multiple Grief

What I had feared had happened to me. What I had dreaded has come to be. I have no peace, no quietness. I have no rest instead only trouble comes.   *Job 3:25-26 (NLT)*

Many people, at any age, can suffer multiple losses, some in a short amount of time. My brother, Howard Campbell Morgan, suffered multiple losses in a short span of time. Let him share a small part of his story and what he experienced and learned from the dying.

"Death welcomes us all at a time and place not of our own choosing. More often than not, especially in terminal illnesses, death comes to us as a friend and companion, to help us prepare for the next step in our journey.

"In the past few years I have been privileged to accompany a wife and a daughter through the 'valley of the shadow of death,' as they feared no evil.

"Especially with my wife, Judith, who died quickly of advanced ovarian cancer, I learned much about the essence of life while I helped her finish her life. Judith showed great courage through intense pain in facing her death given that she so much wanted to experience her children and grandchildren.

"Most beautiful of all, the two of us had time in the evenings to remember our special lives together. These were moments of unbounded joy. She was able to counsel me on how to go on and live a happy life even without her. One day, near the end of her life, we agreed that there was both everything and nothing more to be said, except that we loved each other so much and had been so fortunate to have found each other.

"In my experience, whether it be the case of my wife, Pat; my daughter, Kim; my sister, Mary Ann; my stepmother, Kax; or my mother-in-law, Thelma; *all within two years of each other*, all have been intensely sad in that I cannot speak to them again or hear their voices. But, in the death of loved ones, the only real and meaningful question that has value from the deaths of loved ones is, 'What have I learned from being so close to one dying?'

"I have been given a great gift. In being with a loved one dying, all the facades of the unneeded are dropped; the real life sources surface as cleanly as a pure mountain stream. Death becomes a true friend, an enabler to help one move on where pain and suffering are no more, and a new, eternal dawn of indescribably perfect dimensions has arrived."

Those Difficult First Days

Love is stronger than death. Death has its moments in our lives and in history, but death does not have the last word. It is not easy to speak of love when death seems dominant. But if love is not stronger than death, then whom we cherish most are wrong. . . . We cannot accept this. Even though life seems unfair and all too short, it is better to live as if love is stronger than death.

John C. Morgan

We seek not death, but still we climb the stairs
*   where death is one wide landing to the rooms above.*

George MacDonald

I was like Peter when he began to sink.
To Thee a new prayer therefore I have got—
That, when Death comes in earnest at my door,
Thou wouldst theyself go, when the latch doth clink,
And lead him to my room, up to my cot;
Then hold Thy child's hand, hold and leave him not,
Till Death has done with him for evermore.

George MacDonald

Between Death and Resurrection

The women who had come with him from Galilee followed, and they saw the tomb and how his body was laid. Then they returned, and prepared spices and ointments. On the Sabbath day they rested according to the commandments. *Luke 23:55-56*

The initial shock has dissolved. Now there is no way to deny the loss. All the thank you notes have been written, and you find yourself in a strange limbo between death and the future. You can't help but still grieve the loss. All the years you had with the person reoccur in dreams and thoughts.

The women who loved Jesus were devastated by his horrific death. They prepared to anoint his body, but had to wait since it was the Sabbath. We live on the right side of the resurrection so it is difficult for us to identify with those mourners. Some may have gone back to the room where they saw phantom shadows on the floor, a basin of water, and walls that reverberated with memories of that last meal with Jesus. Did it really happen or did they imagine it? Most of the eleven were in hiding, frightened by reprisals engineered by Jesus's enemies. Maybe some of the disciples huddled in a home and tried to remember stories about Jesus.

In this interim between death and resurrection, those early followers of Jesus had no idea he would rise on the third day. Jesus had told them he would, but they never truly heard him. When they heard the news that Jesus had risen, Luke tells us "They disbelieved for joy" (Luke 24:41).

In your grief, as you live out the long days between your loved one's death and a future reunion, Black Saturday can have meaning for you. Like those early disciples, you too feel forsaken, abandoned, lost. The one you loved will never return. It is like being with them at the fork of a road, and they take one road and you another. You wave good-bye and realize you will never see them again. Mourn for your loved one, and then wait for the first day of the rest of time.

Gracious God, we can identify with those first disciples who thought their world had ended at the cross. Losing a dear one makes us feel that our world has ended and we can't go on. Give us hope there is a third day.

Professionals talk too much about adjustment. I want to emphasize mourning as affirmation. To mourn what has passed, either through illness or death, affirms the life that has been led. To adjust too rapidly is to treat the loss as simply an incident from which one can bounce back; it devalues whom or what has been lost. . . . When a caregiver suffers the death of the person he has cared for, the loss must be mourned fully and in its own time. Only through this mourning can we find a life on the other side of loss.

Arthur W. Frank

Today's society expects those grieving to be stoic and brave, a public display of deep feelings is a source of embarrassment. As a result, feelings are suppressed and leads to depression . . . persons should be encouraged to talk about their grief and express their feelings. Moments of panic, dizziness and hysteria are some of the symptoms of true grief. When these feelings are ventilated or shared with others, they are less frightening.

John C. Morgan and Richard L. Morgan

It Is Okay to Grieve

Grieve, not as those who have no hope.
1 Thessalonians 4:13

Blessed are those who mourn, for they shall be comforted.
Matthew 5:4

Paul's words about grief can be greatly misunderstood. Some read his words this way, "Grieve not, as those who have no hope." This sounds like the Stoics who bore their grief with no sign of emotion. I suggest we move the comma after the first word, so that it reads, "Grieve, not as those who have no hope." Grief is necessary, but there is hope for reunion with lost ones.

People are often still conditioned by societal customs to believe that grief should be suppressed, not expressed. How often you hear these comments when death comes: "Isn't she strong? She is so brave not to cry."

Robert Kavanaugh in his book, *Facing Death,* suggests seven stages of grief: shock, disorganization, volatile emotions, loss, loneliness, relief, and reestablishment. These stages do not necessarily happen in sequence, and overlapping or duplication may occur.

Shock is the initial reaction to loss, as the mind blocks the reality of death. *Disorientation* follows, where the grieving person becomes confused and life seems out of whack. *Volatile emotions*, such as excessive crying or outbursts of anger, is followed by *loss* and *loneliness,* as the full impact of the loss is felt and life goes on without the loved one. In time, *relief* and *reestablishment* come, and life moves on. Some get stuck in the earlier stages and never recover. Others forge a new life too quickly and their grief surfaces later.

One man, who lost his wife from cancer, expressed it this way, "There is no magic wand or protective shield to insulate you from your pain. I am working through it, facing it head on, and now it feels like I do have a future hope, not just a dead past."

Jesus, a man of sorrows and acquainted with grief, you had your moments when grief overcame you. Jerusalem rejected you, a chosen disciple betrayed you, a close friend denied you, and you grieved for their blindness. This gives us assurance that you can bear our grief and help us through it.

O joy that seekest me through pain,
I cannot close my eyes to thee;
I trace the rainbow through the rain,
and feel the promise is not vain.
that morn shall tearless be.

George Matheson

In the depths of winter
I finally realized
That deep within me
There lay an invincible summer.

Albert Camus

Winter Grief: The Mourning After

You have fixed all the bounds of the earth;
  you have created summer and winter.
Psalm 74:17

For now the winter is past,
  the rain is over and gone.
The flowers appear on the earth;
  the time of singing has come.
Song of Songs 2:11

When things settle down after the death of a loved one, we try to get back into our normal routine. However, try as we do to stay busy and active, feelings of grief cling to us like the shells of a young chick. It was the poet, Alexander Pope who wrote, "Grieve for an hour, perhaps, then mourn a year." Although there is no timetable for grief, mourning may last for a long time.

I like to think of those days as winter grief. Winter is the time when all the colors have vanished, and everything is reduced to gray or white. The ground is frozen and still. An eerie silence seems to prevail as life takes on a sadness of farewell. Winter grief is like that. Like animals who hibernate in winter, grieving people often withdraw into themselves and mourn in silence.

However, the word *mourn* comes from the Portugese word *sundade,* a kind of bittersweet sorrow. As Shakespeare wrote, "Farewell is such a sweet sadness." Despite the sadness and endless winter of grief, there are blessings too. Being forced to go inside of ourselves in the silence may be a time of incredible growth; we can spend precious time in contemplation and prayer.

Winter grief is cyclical, it is not restricted to one time. The poet Shelley wrote, "Ah, woe is me! Winter is come and gone. But grief returns with the revolving year." Time can help to ease the pain, but cannot heal the loss.

Yet spring will come. It was in the spring of the year that Christ burst the tomb of winter and dissolved the cold in the warmth of resurrection. Easter says that love is more powerful than death and bigger than cancer.

God of all seasons, we have felt the sting of winter's deaths, now grant us the victory of spring's Resurrection.

And this word: Thou shalt be overcome,
was said full clearly and full mightily,
for assuredness and comfort against
all tribulations that may come.
He said not: Thou shalt not be tempested,
thou shalt not be travailed,
thou shalt not be afflicted,
but He said, Thou shalt not be overcome. . . .
For He loveth and enjoyeth us, and so willeth
He that we loveth and enjoy Him
and mightily trust in Him; and all shall be well.

Julian of Norwich

It is better to grieve than not to grieve. Grief at least tells me that
I was not always what I am now. I was once selected for happiness
—let the memory of that abide me.

   You pass by an old ruined house in a desolate land and do not
heed it—but if you hear that house is haunted by a wild and
beautiful spirit, it acquired an interest and beauty all its own.

Mary Shelley

Grief Never Moves in a Straight Line

He was despised and rejected by others; a man of sorrows and
acquainted with infirmity.   *Isaiah 53:3*

Everyone grieves in their own way. Some prefer to keep their grief within themselves, and share it with no one. Others need to ventilate their sorrow
with a family member or trusted friend. Stages of grief tend to fluctuate. Just
when you think your grief has ended a birthday, anniversary, or special
weekend reminds you of your loved one.

C. S. Lewis kept a journal after the death of his wife, which he later published under the title, *A Grief Observed*. If you want to read and reread one
book on grief, I recommend this classic. Lewis claims that grief is like a long
valley where you are presented with the same country you thought you left
miles ago. There are partial recurrences, but the stages of grief don't repeat
themselves in any sequence. Rabbi Grollman writes, "The reactions of grief
are not like recipes, which give ingredients and certain results. Each person
mourns in a different way."

My father died in 1979. Years later on my father's birthday, October 20, 1992,
he was far from my thoughts as I drove to preach in a small country church in
North Carolina. Suddenly, the radio station began been playing the Irish melody,
"Danny Boy." This was my father's favorite song and one he often sang at the
church. Tears rolled down my cheeks as I realized how much I missed him.

Jesus was a "man of sorrows, acquainted with infirmities." We are given
accounts of when he grieved over how the crowds followed him only
because he did miracles, how the religious rulers resented him, and the pain
and agony of his struggle in Gethsemane. Finally, he bore the tortures of the
damned as he endured the cross, and the unspeakable weight of grief for
those "who knew not what they did."

Grief never moves in a straight line. Ultimately, we move through the
grieving process in God's timing, and always the Spirit of God, the Comforter,
is working for renewal and resurrection.

*Help us, O Comforter Spirit, to rely on you when we grief over our losses
reoccurs. May we take comfort in the fact that although the wound will always
be there, it does get better as we find our strength in your presence.*

When peace, like a river, attendeth my way,
When sorrows like sea billows roll;
Whatever my lot, Thou hast taught me to say,
It is well, it is well, with my soul.

Though Satan should buffet though trials should come,
Let this blest assurance control.
That Christ has regarded my helpless estate,
And hath shed His own blood for my soul.
It is well, it is well, with my soul.

For me, be it Christ, hence to live: be it Christ
If Jordan above me shall roll,
No pang shall be mine, for in death as in life,
Thou wilt whisper Thy peace to my soul.

Horatio Spafford

When the Waves Break

Deep calls to deep at the thunder of your cataracts
all your waves and billows have gone over me.
Psalm 42:7

But by that time the boat, battered by the waves, was far from the land,
for the wind was against them.   *Matthew 14:24*

She was always quiet, reserved, and pleasant toward everyone. She hardly ever expressed feelings and seemed to be such a controlled and confident person. One day, in a church group we were discussing loss and grief, when this lady suddenly burst into loud tears and seemed inconsolable. When she regained her composure she told us, "Today is our anniversary. He died three years ago and I thought I had grieved a long time ago. But remembering our marriage made it seem like a tidal wave had rolled over me." Grief is often like that. Just when you think the storm is over and life has regained some semblance of normalcy, grief descends like a massive ocean wave.

Rabbi Earl Grollman expressed it well. "The death has struck like a tidal wave. You are cut loose from your moorings. You are all but drowning in the sea of your private sorrow. The person who has been a part of your life is gone forever." The writer of Psalm 42 was exiled in the territory where the Jordan River had its origin, to the north of the Hermon Range. As he watched the thundering of the mountain waterfalls, it reminded him of the deep waters through which he was passing.

One of the realities of grief is that it may reoccur at any time. It could be Christmas when you are painfully aware of the loss of a loved one who used to share presents under the Christmas tree. Or, like the woman in our church group, the waves of grief might overwhelm you on your anniversary. Or it could be a song that reminds you of the one you loved.

A sudden storm broke out on the sea of Galilee, and the disciples were terrified. But just as the first streaks of dawn began to appear, Jesus appeared, walking toward them on the water and saying, " Take heart, it is I; be not afraid."

When the waves of sorrow threaten to overwhelm us, send your presence, O Christ. Calm our fears and remind us that the dawn does come.

Sometime at eve when the tide is low,
I shall slip my moorings and sail away,
With no response to the friendly hail
Of kindred craft in the busy bay—
In the silent hush of the twilight pale.
When the night stoops down to embrace the day
And the voices call o'er the waters flow—
Sometime at evening when the tide is low
I shall slip my moorings and sail away.

A few who has watched me sail away
Will miss my craft from the busy bay,
Some friendly barks that were anchored near,
Some loving hearts that my soul held dear.
In silent sorrow shall drop a tear.
But I shall have peacefully furled my sail
In moorings sheltered from storm and gale
And greeted friends who have sailed before
O'er the Unknown sea to the Well Known Shore.

From a fishing village in Cape Cod

There is a sacredness in tears. They are not the mark of
weakness, but of power. They speak more eloquently than
ten thousand tongues. They are messengers of overwhelming
grief, of deep contrition, and of unspeakable love.

Washington Irving

Cry Your Heart Out

The king was deeply moved and went up to the chamber over the gate and began to weep.

1 Samuel 18:33a

Jesus began to weep.

John 11:35

In our western culture we still believe people ought not to cry in public. Some who do cry are often embarrassed and quickly try to cover their tears. Most men do not cry very often, and even if they do, they believe it is a sign of weakness. As children, some men were told, "Brave boys don't cry." So people often stifle their tears and cry inside of themselves.

David, a strong male king, burst into loud weeping when he heard that his beloved son, Absalom, was dead. His grief was so intense that the historian could never forget his words, "O Absalom, my son, my son!" David's grief was not only for his son, but also because Absalom's death meant the end of his dreams for his son as his successor.

The strong Son of God also wept loudly when his friend Lazarus died. The rest of the mourners wept without hope. I don't think Jesus wept for Lazarus, whom he would bring back from the tomb, but he grieved *with* Mary and Martha. Jesus showed his compassion and humanity in those tears. Shakespeare wrote, "To weep is to make less the depth of grief."

An American poet, Ted Rosenthal, was told he had leukemia and was going to die in a short time. Facing his death, Rosenthal wrote these words: But, first, that's alright, go ahead and cry / Cry, cry, cry your heart out. / It's love. . . . / O, I am weeping, but it's stage center for / all of us.

Scientists tell us that people who are able to cry enjoy better mental and emotional health. So, don't stifle your tears. Let them flow!

Come, ye disconsolate, where'er ye languish. Come to the mercy seat, fervently kneel. Here bring your wounded hearts, here tell your anguish. Earth has no sorrows that heaven cannot heal (Thomas Moore).

O Lord, why do you stand so far away?
Why did you hide when I need you the most?

Psalm 10:1 (NLT)

O Lord, how long will you forget me? Forever?
How long will you look the other way?
How long must I struggle with anguish in my soul,
*   with sorrow in my heart every day?*

Psalm 13:1-2a (NLT)

My God, my God! Why have you forsaken me?
Why do you remain so distant?
Why do you ignore my cries for help?
Every day I call to you, my God, but you do not answer.
Every night you hear my voice, but I find no relief.

Psalm 22:1-2 (NLT)

Does God realize what is going on? . . .
Is the Most High even aware of what is happening?

Psalm 73:11 (NLT)

O Lord, I cry out to you. I will keep on pleading day by day.
O Lord, why do you reject me? Why do you turn your face
away from me?

Psalm 88:13 (NLT)

Anger Is Healthy

Martha said to Jesus, "Lord, if you had been here, my brother would not have died. . . ." When Mary came where Jesus was and saw him she knelt at his feet, and said to him, "Lord, if you had been here, my brother would not have died."

John 11:32-33

After their brother Lazarus died, Mary and Martha both expressed their grief when they saw Jesus, and their words were tinged with anger. They knew Jesus's power to heal the sick, why hadn't he saved their brother?

When you lose a loved one, it is natural to be angry. Sometimes we vent our anger at the one who died. How well I remember standing with a new widow at the funeral home. As she glanced at her husband in the coffin, who had died from a sudden stroke, she said to me, "The nerve of him to die and leave us like this."

At other times we get angry at God and cry out, "How could you let this happen, God?" We need to realize that this is normal, and God understands. Others may vent their anger at the doctor or we may internalize our anger and torment ourselves with such thoughts as, "Why didn't I insist she see a doctor earlier," or "If only I had spent more time with him instead of devoting so much time to the children."

In my youth I was taught that expressing anger was sinful, despite Paul word's, "Be angry, but do not sin" (Ephesians 4:26). So I kept my anger inside, bottled up my feelings, and wore a happy face. Internalized anger leads to depression, and it took intensive therapy for me to learn to release my anger. Now we are taught to express our anger: some scream, whack pillows with a tennis racket, or slam doors. Neither extreme is healthy. It is far better to talk with a counselor or friend, or express anger to God as the patriarch Job and the psalmists did.

Rabbi Earl Grollman expresses my feelings when he writes, "Resentment is a moral part of your grief process. As your pain subsides, so will your anger."

Dearest Friend, you got angry when God was misrepresented or people were mistreated. I also get angry—at you or others or myself with the loss of this loved one. Be patient with me now, Jesus, for I am really angry.

47

Again at Christmas did we weave
The holly round the Christmas hearth;
The silent snow possess'd the earth,
And calmly fell our Christmas-eve.

The yule-log sparkled keen with frost,
No wing of wind the region swept,
But over all things brooding slept
The quiet sense of something lost.

Alfred Lord Tennyson

At Easter time you feel it most,
the loss of someone gone before,
as if you could rejoice at all—
though everyone else thinks otherwise.
You only know the emptiness
of hollow hymns and happiness
and sermons full of liveliness.
Every closet tells a tale,
every item brings to mind
the memory of a loss so deep
that all you want to do is sleep
away the waking hours
and dull the dread you feel inside.
The prayer is simple, said anew:
Let me make it through the day.

John C. Morgan

Silent Night, Lonely Night

> This child is destined for the falling and rising of many in Israel and to be a sign that will be opposed; so that the inner thoughts of many will be revealed and a sword will pierce your own soul too.
> *Luke 2:34-35*

It was the first Christmas season and a woman whose husband had died some months ago expressed her feelings in the following way:

> It's the first week of Advent and everywhere I go I hear Christmas music and see signs of the season—happy, excited faces of children and those endless parties. I dread going alone to the candlelight Christmas eve service without Jack. For me it is not silent night, holy night, but silent night, *lonely* night. I just want to hide in my apartment until the season is over. Everything reminds me of Jack.

We continue to romanticize Christmas and focus only on peace and good will. But it can be a terribly lonely time for those who have lost loved ones. I visited a widow who talked about how difficult Christmas still was for her, even though it had been several years since her husband's death. Grief does come in cycles, and the holidays and anniversaries are especially rough times. As we sat in a grief group a few days before Christmas, I thought to myself, grief is like being in a house and suddenly a window opens and cold air pours into the room and you shiver. You get up and shut the window. It may open again, but finally it stays shut and you forget it ever happened. One member of the group had a positive approach. She said, "It's been ten years since Harry died. I have changed some of the ways I celebrate Christmas and moved on. I invite some other widows to share Christmas dinner with me, and we even exchange presents. But their presence is the real gift to me. The alternative is to sit around and pity yourself forever."

O Holy Child of Bethlehem for whom there was no room in Bethlehem's Inn, you can share our pain at Christmas, as we mourn our loved ones. May your presence bring tidings of comfort and joy which the world cannot give or take away.

I am reminded of C. S. Lewis's experience of tramping through thickly forested woods. He notes how patches of bright sunlight occasionally break through the dark coolness of the environment. *Rays suddenly break through the branches and strike the hiker with feelings of warmth and life. He suggests an analogy with spiritual* "patches of Godlight" *that we spontaneously experience as we walk in the shadowy woods of life and death.*

Donald E. Messer, italics added

The one thing that should never be said when someone dies is, "It is the will of God." My own consolation lies in knowing that it was not *the will of God that Alex die; that when the waves closed over the sinking car, God's heart was the first of all our hearts to break.*

William Sloane Coffin, from a sermon preached ten years after the death of his son

Where Are You, God?

My God, my God! Why have you forsaken me?
Why do you remain so distant?
Why do you ignore my cries for help?
Every day I call to you, my God, but you do not answer.
Every night you hear my voice, but I find no relief.

Psalm 22:1, 2 (NLT)

As time goes on, some mourners begin to question their faith. They often ask God why this happened, and why didn't God answer their prayers for their loved one? They may go through a time of the "dark night of the soul" when God seems absent and far away.

Jesus experienced this kind of abandonment at the cross. He must have had Psalm 22 on his mind as he cried, "My God, my God, why have you forsaken me?" in such a way that the Gospel writers even record the Aramaic words he spoke. No words in Scripture are more clouded in horror and mystery than this cry of anguish. Here is suffering beyond description, so terrible that heaven itself drew a veil over the scene. "Darkness came over the whole land until three in the afternoon" (Matthew 27:45).

Elizabeth Barrett Browning caught a glimpse of what this all means in her words:

Yea, once Emmanuel's orphaned cry
His universe hath shaken,
It went up single, echoless,
My God, I am forsaken.

It went up from his holy lips
Amid his lost creation,
That no one else need ever
Cry that cry of desolation.

We may feel God has forgotten us, we may feel helpless at things we don't understand, we may feel God is absent, but the comfort is that there is no place where we have to go where Christ has not gone before. We, too, have every right to cry, "My God, my God, why?" God understands and in the darkness watches over us.

Holy Jesus, there was no suffering like yours. Yet there are times I wonder where God was when my loved one died, and where God is now. I sit silently in the darkness.

It should be clear by now that grief is a process. . . .
Grief does not stay the same from day to day or week to week.
It changes. It is like a journey down a winding road. . . .
We must first grieve the loss. Before we can go forward
we must go backward. Grieving comes first. Grieving makes
growing possible.

R. Scott Sullender

I know not what the future hath
Of marvel or surprise,
Assured along that life and death
His mercy overlies.

And if my heart and flesh are weak
To bear an untried pain
The bruised reed He will not break,
But strengthen and sustain.

I know not where His islands lift
Their fronded palms in air;
I only know I cannot drift
Beyond His love and care.

John Greenleaf Whittier

Through the Valley

Even though I walk
    through the darkest valley,
I fear no evil,
    for you are with me;
your rod and your staff—
    they comfort me.   *Psalm 23:4*

Theologian Joseph Sittler has pointed out that "You walk through the valley of the *shadow* of death—not the valley of death. The valley of death is constituted by the moment of death, but for all of life one walks through the valley over which the *shadow* of death moves. . . . The whole of life is lived under the shadow of death."

In this classic description of God's loving care in Psalm 23, David reviewed his life through the image of the shepherd and the sheep. He reflected on his earlier days as a shepherd boy in the Judean hills, and realized that God cares for us as the shepherd cares for the sheep. The sheep are guided through the shadows of dark ravines, where certain death from wolves is ever present. The shepherd uses his rod to ward off the wolves, and the crook of his staff to catch any sheep that wander too near the edge of a cliff. In our shadows of life, especially when we grieve the loss of a loved one, God rescues us from despair and spiritual death. God leads us *through* the valley of the shadows. We will encounter these dark moments of doubt and despair, but God preserves us from going off the deep end and losing our faith.

Valleys are created by the peaks of mountains. As you emerge from the valley, the grandeur of mountain peaks come into view. There is sunshine and beauty. So Psalm 23 ends with a burst of optimism, "Surely, goodness and mercy shall follow me all the days of my life, and I shall dwell in the house of the Lord forever." Despite the agonizing losses of loved ones, we are promised the presence of the One who comes to our side in these valleys of shadow, and we do not need to be afraid.

Many people have memorized the 23rd Psalm. In a quiet place pray the words of the Psalm. Hold some loved one you have lost before your eyes, and let the Psalm speak its own word to your heart.

Life Begins Again

In Celtic lore also, there is a strong conviction that the dead are not far away. The Irish tradition holds that this world and the eternal world are interwoven. . . . The vein between the two worlds is very thin now and friends from the eternal world come to take a person home. . . . In Ireland there is the tradition called caosindeadh. *These are the people, usually women, who come to mourn the dead person. With high-pitched wailing they tell the story of the person's life, a sad and beautiful gathering of key events, a narrative filled with the immense loneliness of loss.*

Kathleen R. Fischer

Preserve the Memories

Now on that same day two of them were going to a village named Emmaus, about seven miles from Jerusalem and talking with each other about all these things that had happened.

Luke 24:13-14

Two people walked the seven lonely miles from Jerusalem to Emmaus. They talked about the tragic death of Jesus on the cross, of course, but I can also imagine they began recalling some of Jesus's stories. They reminded themselves of how Jesus loved to hang out with tax collectors and sinners, and never refused anyone who came for healing or help. Imagine how that stranger who was the risen Lord must have inwardly smiled.

When a loved one dies, it is appropriate to preserve our memories of them. Often we revisit significant places where we went with them, or moments when we shared some of life's greatest joys: a birthday party for a child, a high school graduation, a wedding. Our eyes tear up as their presence becomes so real. That is the way it ought to be. John O'Donohue wrote, "Where does the soul of a person go when the person dies? . . . It can be nowhere but here . . . the eternal world does not seem to be a place but a different state of being . . . the dead are with us."

Cleophas and his companion suddenly became aware that this stranger was different. Why, it was almost as if Rabbi Jesus was again explaining the Torah and the New Commandment. But it was at a simple supper in Emmaus when he broke bread, that they realized it was Jesus, now risen from the dead. Memory had become reality. As we preserve the memories of our loved ones, not just at the time of their deaths, but all times, they are with us in the world of the spirit, and we await the glorious reunion when we will see them again in the eternal world.

"O Jesus, ever with us stay. Make all our moments calm and bright. Chase the dark night of sin away. Shed o'er the world thy holy light." Lord, we pray that his ancient prayer by Bernard of Clairvaux would kindle hope in us as the presence of Christ made the hearts of those disciples burn within them on the road. May the light of hope break through the darkness of our grief.

The melody that the loved one played upon the piano of our life will never be played that way quite again, but we must close the keyboard and allow the instrument to gather dust. We must seek out other artists, new friends who gradually will help us to find the road to life again, who will walk on that road with us.

Joshua Loth Liebman

For what is it to die but to stand naked in the wind and to melt into the sun? . . . And when you have reached the mountain top, then you shall begin to climb. And when the earth shall claim your limbs, then you shall truly dance.

Kahlil Gibran

What to Do with Those Things?

> There was a believer in Joppa named Dorcas. . . . She was always
> doing kind things for others and helping the poor. About this time she
> became ill and died. Her friends prepared her for burial and laid her in an
> upstairs room. As soon as Peter arrived they took him to the upstairs room.
> The room was filled with widows who were weeping and showing the
> coats and garments Dorcas had made for them.
>
> *Acts 9:36-37 (NLT)*

When Dorcas died, her friends sent for Peter, and he went to the upstairs room where she was laid out. Her friends showed Peter the clothes she had made for them, and wondered what they should do with her things. Give them to the poor? Take them to the Joppa Goodwill Center? One of the most difficult tasks of the survivor is to have to clear out the deceased person's wardrobe and other belongings. There are two extremes to avoid.

On the one hand, it is not wise to be impulsive and try to clear out everything that reminds you of your grief. On the other hand, holding on to clothes and possessions can also stifle grief. I know a woman who kept her husband's fishing rod and shotgun in the corner of her apartment exactly where he left them before his death. All she did was dust them once in a while. Such acts prolong an unnatural attachment to the deceased person, and prolongs the grief process.

A happy medium needs to be found. I like to imagine that some of the widows kept some of those clothes Dorcas made and wore them in her memory. Maybe the Christians of Joppa gave clothes to others, since Dorcas's life was a ministry to the poor. There is no prescribed timetable or proper schedule for disposing of the belongings of our loved ones after their deaths. When the time is right, exercise caution that honors their requests, be kind to yourself, and have no regrets.

Savior Christ, at your death all you left was a seamless robe, woven by your mother. We come into this world with little but ourselves, and all we have and own are left to others. Grant us wisdom to know the right time and to do the proper thing with what we own, and what our loved ones leave us.

There is a balm in Gilead
To make the wounded whole;
There is balm in Gilead
To heal the sin-sick soul.

Sometimes I feel discouraged
And think my work's in vain,
But then the Holy Spirit
Revives my soul again.

There is a balm in Gilead,
To make the wounded whole;
There is a balm in Gilead
To heal the sin-sick soul.

       African-American Spiritual

Perhaps they are not the stars,
but rather openings in heaven
where the love of our lost ones pours through
and shines down upon us to let us know
they are happy.

        Inspired by Inuit Legend

There Is Balm in Gilead

Is there no balm in Gilead?
Is there no physician there?
Why then has the health of my poor
      people not been restored?   *Jeremiah 8:22*

The prophet Jeremiah is known as "the weeping prophet." He deeply felt the serious problems his nation faced and knew that judgment was imminent.

Balm was a healing salve that came from Gilead. But there was no balm or physician to heal Judah's brokenness. Jeremiah wondered if there was any hope for the beleaguered nation, any meaning which could be derived from the disaster soon to strike his people. Soon his cries of judgment would become words of hope beyond despair.

When death robs us of a loved one, we feel heartbroken and also wonder, "Is there any balm in Gilead?" Our security has been shattered by our loss, and we face a grim future.

Years ago a woman who suffered the loss of her husband, and then the tragic shooting of her son, shared this poem with me.

TWO BOXES

I have in hand two boxes
which God gave me to hold.
God said, "Put all your sorrows
    in the black,
and all your joys in the gold."
I heeded the words and in the
    two boxes
both my joys and sorrows I stored.

But though the gold became heavier
    each day,
the black was as light as before. . . .
I asked, "Why give me the boxes
with the gold and the black
    and the hole?"
"My child," God said, "the gold is
for you to count your blessings,
the black is for you to let go."

Gracious God, life has not always been blue skies and brilliant sunshine; at times we have known dark clouds of troubles and the darkness of pain. But if we give you those dark moments we can believe Jesus's words, "Be of good cheer, for I have overcome the world."

Part of what has had you holding on so desperately
is the fear that if you let go, you would lose that person forever.
Now you begin to glimpse the possibilities of being with him or her
in a new way. If you loosen the sad grip of grief, a new belonging
becomes possible between you.

John O'Donohue

If you free what is inside you, it will make you free.
But if you hold on to what is inside you, it will destroy you.

Zen Proverb

When one door closes, another opens,
but we often look so long
and regretfully upon the closed door,
we do not see the ones which open for us.

Alexander Graham Bell

Letting Go

Jesus turned to her and said, "Mary." She turned to him and said, "Rabbouni." Jesus said to her, "Do not hold on to me, because I have not yet ascended to my father."

John 20:16-17

When Mary finally recognized Jesus and called him, "Rabbouni," she was still clinging to the Jesus of Nazareth whom she knew. She still thought of him as "My Teacher," or "My Master." She reached out to touch him, but Jesus drew back, and said, "Do not hold on to me." Jesus had not returned to resume his former way of life that she knew. She had to learn a new relationship—that he would be a constant presence in her heart versus a physical reality.

Grief is an attachment; letting go of a loved one is difficult. Some do get stuck in the past and never give up that attachment. Like Gulliver, tied to the ground with stakes and ropes by the Lilliputians, we have thousands of ties binding them to a lost love one.

These ties can become neurotic. I remember a widow in my church whose husband was cremated, and she kept the urn with his remains on the dining table (as if he was still eating with her). It took some gentle persuasion for her to surrender that ritual and allow me to perform the scattering of the ashes. Only then could she find closure and move on with her life.

Like Mary Magdalene, we have to let go of our attachment to the person who has died, so we can realize that our connection now is spiritual, not physical. Our grief reaches denouement when we say good-bye, and wish our loved ones Godspeed on their journey to eternity. In a real sense, we are saying good-bye to our old way of relating, and hello to a new connection with them.

Father of lights, with whom there is no variation or shadow due to change, teach us that we are ghosts in this life and our loved ones in glory shine. Give us a sense of their presence now in this life and the hope we shall see them again in heaven.

As every flower fades and all youth
Departs, so life at every stage,
So every virtue, so our grasp of truth,
Blooms in its day and may not last forever.
Since life may summon us at every age
Be ready, heart, for parting, new endeavor,
Be ready bravely and without remorse
To find new light that old ties cannot give.
In all beginnings dwells a magic force
For guarding us and helping us to live.

Hermann Hesse

God of the coming years,
*   through paths unknown;*
We follow Thee;
When we are strong, Lord, leave us not alone.
Be Thou for us in life our daily bread,
Our heart's truer home
*   when all our days have sped.*

Hugh Thompson Kerr

Moving On

I am about to do a new thing, now it springs forth,
      do you not perceive it?
I will make a way in the wilderness
      and rivers in the desert.

Isaiah 43:19

The Lord our God spoke to us at Horeb, saying, "You have stayed long enough at this mountain. Resume your journey."

Deuteronomy 1:6-7a

Twice in Israel's history God charged the children of Israel to let go of the past and move into a new future. For Moses and the Israelites, it meant giving up their wilderness existence, and moving forward. For the Hebrew people in exile, it was high time to stop clinging to their life in Babylon, for God was going to make a way in the wilderness, a new exodus.

Losses in life do plunge us into mourning and sadness. But the days come that is the end of the beginning. Ann Dawson writes, "But it does get easier. Eventually, gradually, I began to realize that life does resume some semblance of normalcy. I found myself having more good days than bad ones. I knew that the sad feelings wouldn't last forever, and that life could again be enjoyed."

No one can tell anyone when the moment of new beginnings come. At times it is just a feeling that despite everything that has happened, life will be okay. At other times the new day dawns with a new relationship which brings joy to your life.

Rabbi Joshua Loth Liebman uses the metaphor of playing the piano to show the need to move on with life. The melody that the loved one played upon the piano of our life will never be played quite that way again. But we can't shut down the keyboard and get stuck in our grief. Other tunes can be played . . . in God's time.

We are so much like the blind man at Bethsaida, dear God. We see life, but not with clear vision. Often we can't believe in a bright future because of a dark past. Open our eyes to a new beginning where the past is cherished, and the future embraced.

65

The coin of life is stamped with death
so that what we buy will be truly precious.

Rabindranath Tagore

O Master, let me walk with Thee
In lowly paths of service free;
Tell me Thy secret; help me bear
The strain of toil, the fret of care.
Teach me Thy patience, still with Thee
In closer, dearer company,
In work that keeps faith sweet and strong,
In trust that triumphs over wrong.

Washington Gladden

Make Each Day Count

So teach us to count our days
that we may gain a wise heart.
Psalm 90:12

The psychologist Abraham Maslow recovered from a massive coronary attack, and called the recovery, "the post-mortem life." He described this life in these words, "The confrontation with death—and the reprieve from it—makes everything so precious, so beautiful, so cared for, that I feel more strongly than ever the impulse to embrace it and let myself be overwhelmed by it." Although Maslow died in 1970 at the age of sixty-two, his last years found him leaving a rich legacy on how to live a self-actualized life.

This is not only true for survivors who consider every new day as "gravy," but also for those who have lost loved ones. Every day's survival is both a triumph and opportunity to make the day count. This means ignoring little irritants that plague our lives and not wasting time in trivialities. Losing a loved one puts you in touch with the words of James, "How do you know what will happen tomorrow? For your life is like a morning fog that is here for a little while, and then it's gone" (James 4:14, NLT). Life is so uncertain and there are no guarantees.

We realize the sacredness of the present moment. The Indian mystic said it well: "The butterfly counts not minutes, but moments, and has time enough." Survivors who lose a loved one prioritize life and have time for the essentials.

Recently I had the privilege of interviewing a Holocaust survivor, Sam Weinreb. Sam lost his parents and all his brothers and sisters in the death camps of Auschwitz. He is now one of the younger Holocaust survivors who is growing older. Realizing that soon eyewitnesses of this horror will soon be gone, he devotes his time and energy to telling the story, so no one will ever forget it. When I asked this amazing person who has experienced so much loss to summarize his life, he replied, "Don't take life for granted. Live each day to the fullest. Be good to everyone."

God of every person, we never know what a day may bring forth, or when our time will come. May we be grateful for the blessing of each day, and help us to have a heart of wisdom.

When the risen Christ appears to his disciples, they have trouble recognizing him. He is the same Jesus with whom they walked and shared meals, but now somehow so different that they do not know him. Jesus's appearances are like finding an old friend so changed after many years that we walk right past her and do a double take when we slowly realize who she is. In each Easter story there are just such moments of not knowing and then suddenly recognizing Jesus.

Kathleen R. Fischer

And our eyes at last shall see him through his own redeeming love;
for that child so dear and gentle is our Lord in heaven above;
and he leads his children on to the place where he has gone.

Cecil Alexander

The Resurrection Hope

> Blessed be the God and Father of our Lord Jesus Christ! By his great mercy he has given us new birth into a living hope through the resurrection of Jesus Christ from the dead.
>
> *1 Peter 1:3*

The forty days when the risen Lord appeared to his friends are our one hold on eternity. During that time God pulled back the secrecy that shrouds heaven and revealed, for forty days, what heaven would be like. It was a paradox for those first disciples, as it is for us. There was continuity between Jesus of Nazareth and the risen Christ. Yet there was a difference. Christ was transformed into a new dimension, the resurrection body. It was not as if Jesus had gone on a journey and returned the same Jesus who had left. Heaven had broken into our world; eternity into our time. Something marvelous and awesome had happened—God had raised Jesus from the dead.

The Gospels record something the disciples believed was both utterly real and unique. They were convinced that although Jesus was no longer with them in the way he was, nevertheless, he was still with them.

I recently attended a concert where the music was glorious and the solo violinist was out of this world. I saw this as an analogy of the resurrection body. Think of the violin as your body, and the music as your soul. The violin is made to express music, and the body expresses our soul. Even if the violin is broken or damaged, the music is still there. Just suppose the violin was damaged beyond repair and had to be discarded. The musician would then find a new violin, and the music would be resumed. When death destroys this life, God gives us a new instrument, the resurrection body, to make new music. "Then the saying that is written will come true: 'Death has been swallowed up in victory. Where, O death is your victory? Where O death is your sting?' . . . But thanks be to God! He gives us the victory through our Lord Jesus Christ" (1 Corinthians 15:54-55, 57).

Loving Lord who raised Jesus from the dead, lift us from the shadows of this life that we may behold the light of eternity. Grant us faith, that as Jesus conquered death and rose from the grave, so our loved ones though they be dead, yet they are *alive.*

A MEMORIAL PRAYER

We give back to you, O God, those whom you gave to us.
You did not lose them when you gave them to us
  and we do not lose them by their return to you.
Your dear Son has taught us that life is eternal and love cannot die.
So death is only a horizon and a horizon is only the limit of our sight.
Open our eyes to see more clearly, and draw us closer to you
  that we may know that we are nearer to our loved ones,
  who are with you. You have told us that you are preparing
  a place for us; prepare us also for that happy place,
  that where you are, we may also be always,
O dear Lord of life and death.

William Penn

Death is not extinguishing the light;
It is putting out the lamp
because the dawn has come.

Tagore

Will I See Them Again?

> A little while, and you will no longer see me, and again, a little while, and you will see me. . . . Very truly I say unto you, you will weep and mourn, but the world will rejoice; you will have pain, but your pain will turn into joy. *John 16:16, 20*

> Beloved, we are God's children now; what we will be has not yet been revealed. What we do know is this: when he is revealed we will be like him, for we shall see him as he is. *1 John 3:2*

The constant question most asked by those who have lost loved ones is, "Will I see them again?" Alfred Lord Tennyson expressed this universal cry of the human heart in these words:

O that 'twere possible
After long grief and pain
To find the arms of my true love
Round me once again. . . .

Ah Christ, that it were possible
For one short hour to see
The souls we loved, that they might tell us
What and where they be.

The gates guard their secrets well, and few stray beams of light escape through the crevices. Our resurrection hope is that just as Jesus was in those forty days in a new resurrection personality, so our loved one will be in eternity.

The apostle Paul believed that Christ "will change our lowly bodies to be like his glorified body." Our personal reality, our true selves, will be raised to a new life. The ancient Greeks believed that the body was the prison of the soul, and death liberated the spirit from the body. They thought that life after death was as natural a function as waking from sleep. The Christian belief is that when we die, we are truly dead. But in that death God raises us to a new life—what Paul called "the spiritual body." This means we are not talking about these particular cells and chromosomes, which will surely decay to dust. The essential person you were in this life will be transformed with a new "body" for the new life in heaven. And yes, there will be reunion with all those "angel faces, whom we have loved long since, and lost awhile."

Compassionate God, we feebly struggle, they in glory shine. May we see through our tears that our loved ones are safe and secure, at home with you.

While not many of us will be required
  to lay down our lives for Christ . . .
  each of us is asked to lay down our lives
  and become both sacrificial and vulnerable
  in our ministry to others.
This is clearly evident if we seek to use our own pain
  as a tool for coming alongside others who grieve.
We will need to be honest about our failings. . . .
We may be required to talk about details
  in our life that we would rather leave
  in the silence of our memories.
Most painful of all, we will undoubtedly
  be required to cry with others who are grieving
  and absorb their pain into our hearts.

Steve Griffiths

Mourned to Minister

All praise to God the Father of our Lord Jesus Christ. He is the source of every mercy and the God who comforts us. He comforts us in all our troubles so that we can comfort others. When others are troubled, we will be able to give them the same comfort God has given us.

2 Corinthians 1:3-4 (NLT)

It is true that you have to work through your own grief before you can help others in grief. Several years ago I was being supervised in pastoral care, and played a tape of my conversation with a severely depressed man. Suddenly my supervisor said, "Stop the tape!" He went on, "The man was describing his depression after his father's death. You either never heard him, or if you did, you distracted him by changing the subject." I thought for a moment, and then realized why I had blocked out his words. My father had died a few months before this interview, and I had not worked through my grief. I could not relate to my client's death because it was too painful to relive my own loss.

Paul tells the Corinthians that as God has comforted them in their grief, they can offer that same comfort to others. It means keeping the vital balance between *intimacy* and *distance*. We cannot bear people's burdens *for* them, but we can bear their burdens *with* them. It is too easy to lose our own center when we become too absorbed in the pain of others. Drowning with another person is no way to save them.

Be the person who stands in silence at the funeral home, because you once stood there. Be the person who offers the ministry of presence when everyone else leaves, because you remember what that presence meant to you. Be the person who tells the grieving person about a support group, because you remember how much it meant to you. The apostle Paul wrote, "Let each of you look not to his own interests, but to the interests of others" (Philippians 2:4). When you live out Paul's counsel you have learned and grown through your experience. You have become healed victims and wounded healers.

Healer of pain, Comforter of those who mourn, I know that comfort. Now help me to discern where other mourners are, and to reach across the distance and to be a minister of comfort whenever that moment may present itself.

Before Columbus set sail to cross the Atlantic, people believed that the world ended somewhere past Gibraltar. The royal motto said plainly, Ne Plus Ultra, *meaning, "There is no more beyond here." But when Columbus returned, he had actually discovered a whole new world. The ancient motto was now meaningless. Queen Isabella changed the words, simply deleting the* ne *leaving just two words,* Plus Ultra, *or "There is plenty more beyond here."*

Author Unknown

Yesterday is history
Tomorrow is a mystery
Today is a gift—the present.

Eleanor Roosevelt

THIRTIETH DAY

It Does Get Better

When the Lord restored the fortunes of Zion, we were like those who dream. . . . The Lord has done great things for us and we rejoiced. . . . Those who go out weeping . . . shall come home with shouts of joy.
Psalm 126:1, 3, 5

It is one of life's ironies that when people who grieve start to recover they are not always aware that healing is taking place. Monica Dickens, a great-great-granddaughter of Charles Dickens, was widowed after "thirty-four gloriously happy years." Reflecting later on her grief journey, she was surprised to discover she had been making progress toward healing. She shared her insight in this way, "Recovery is not usually that dramatic. Most turning points are slow and tentative. You get a good night's sleep. You bake something, put up a shelf."

The writer of Psalm 126 rejoices at the return of the Hebrew exiles to Jerusalem. His words seem to reflect the Near East custom of weeping at the time of sowing with a view to ensuring the fertility of the seed. The people who once sat down by the rivers of Babylon and wept at their displacement, now could sing with joy at their restoration to their home and temple.

Restoration means we have come to terms with our loss, and on a deeper level, the mystery of life and death. Our questions cannot be fully answered in this nor do we punish ourselves with thoughts of what could have been. We realize there is an overarching meaning to it all, and although, "Now we see imperfectly, as in a poor mirror . . . then we shall see everything with perfect clarity . . . then I will know completely, just as God knows me now" (1 Corinthians 13:12, NLT). We can really believe now that every ending has a new beginning. That is our faith. That is our hope. So we rest in the assurance that "nothing can separate us from the love of God."

Our loving God, we have come to a bend of the road on our grief journey. We have experienced many detours and delays. It may well be that we must now choose the right road for the next step. So we seize the day and live the future in hope.

Acknowledgments

Algeri, Lynn. Poem. Used by Permission.

Burton, John David. "When No One Comes Back from the Cemetery Except Me," from *Naked in the Street*. Copyright © 1985 by John David Burton. Used by permission of the author.

Dawson, Ann. Excerpted from *A Season of Grief*. Copyright © 2002 by Ave Maria Press, PO Box 428, Notre Dame, Ind. 46556. www.avemaria-press.com. Used by permission of the publisher.

De Waal, Esther. *Living with Contradiction*. Copyright © 1989, 1997 by Esther de Waal. Used by permission of Morehouse Publishing.

Fischer, Kathleen R. Extract from *Imaging Life After Death*. Copyright © 2005 by Paulist Press, New York. www.paulistpress.com. Used with permission of Paulist Press.

Frank, Arthur W. Excerpt from *At The Will of the Body*. Copyright © 1991. Used by permission of Arthur W. Frank and Catherine E. Foote. Reprinted by permission of Houghton Mifflin Company. All rights reserved.

Fulton, Maria. "Mourning Glory." Used by permission of the author.

Kahlil Gibran. *The Prophet*. Copyright © 1951 by Alfred A, Knopf. Used by permission of the publisher.

Griffiths, Steve. Extract from *God of the Valley,* pp. 152-53. Copyright © 2002 by BRF Press. Reproduced with permission.

Grollman, Earl A. *Living When a Loved One Has Died*. Copyright © 1995 by Beacon Press. Used by permission of the author and publisher.

Keck, David. *Forgetting Whose We Are: Alzheimer's Disease and the Love of God*. Copyright © 1996 by Abingdon Press. All rights reserved.

MacDonald, George. *Diary of an Old Soul*. Copyright © 1994 by Augsburg Press. Used by permission.

Maxwell, Florida Scott. *The Measure of My Days*. Copyright © 1978 by Alfred A. Knopf. Used by permission.

Messer, Donald E. Messer. "Patches of Sunlight" in *Reflections on Grief and Spiritual Growth*. Copyright © 2005 by Abingdon Press. Used by permission.

Morgan, Howard Campbell. *Meditation on Multiple Grief.* Used by permission of author.

Morgan, John Crossley. *Awakening of the Soul: A Book of Daily Devotions,* edited by John C. Morgan. Copyright © Skinner House. Available at 1-800-215-9072 or www.uua.org/bookstore. Used with permission.

————. "Poem." Used with permission.

———— and Richard L. Morgan. *Psychology of Death and Dying.* Copyright © 1977 by the Authors. Used with permission.

O'Donohue, John. *Eternal Echoes.* Copyright © 1999 by HarperCollins. Used by permission. All rights reserved.

Roussell, Jr., Jeroid O'Neil. *Dealing with Grief: Theirs and Ours.* Copyright © 1999 by Alba House. Used by permission.

Sullender, R. Scott. *Losses in Later Life.* Copyright © 1999 by Haworth Press. Used by permission.

The Author

Richard L. Morgan is a best-selling author who has written and spoken widely on spirituality, aging, and grief. A retired minister and professor, he has also served as a chaplain in a variety of settings including hospitals, nursing homes, and hospices. Among his many publications, he is the author of *No Wrinkles on the Soul, Remembering Your Story,* and *Fire in the Soul* all published with Upper Room Books.

The Herald Press Meditation Books
Over a half million copies in print.

"Wise and relevant."
—*Bookstore Journal*

"Attractively packaged and pleasant."
—*Christian Century*

"This series has been around for a number of years
. . . and captures the spirit of Christian Love."
—*Christian Citizen*

"Wholesome, biblical and practical."
—*Moody Monthly*

"Attractive enough for a Christmas gift
and cherishable any month of the year."
—*The Christian Reader*

"*Meditations for the Grieving* is brilliant,
insightful, and compelling."
—*Dr. Earl A. Grollman*

"Richard Morgan speaks courageously and wisely
to the very depths of our soul."
—*Rev. Martin R. Ankrum*